TIMELINES OF
AMERICAN HISTORY™

A Timeline of the Abolitionist Movement

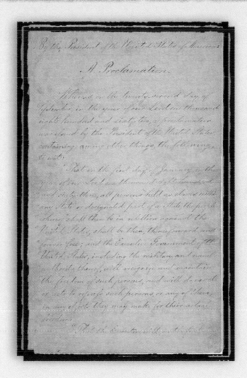

Judy Levin

The Rosen Publishing Group, Inc., New York

For Laura

Published in 2004 by The Rosen Publishing Group, Inc.
29 East 21st Street, New York, NY 10010

Copyright © 2004 by The Rosen Publishing Group, Inc.

First Edition

Library of Congress Cataloging-in-Publication Data
Levin, Judy, 1978–
A timeline of the abolitionist movement / Judy Levin—1st ed.
p. cm. — (Timelines of American history)
Includes bibliographical references and index.
ISBN 0-8239-4537-5 (lib. bdg.)
1. Antislavery movements—United States—History—Chronology—Juvenile literature. 2. Abolitionists—United States—History—Chronology—Juvenile literature. 3. Slavery—United States—History—Chronology—Juvenile literature. 4. African Americans—History—Chronology—Juvenile literature. I. Title. II. Series.
E441.L47 2004

2003021049

On the cover: A celebration of the Thirteenth Amendment, which ended slavery in 1865
On the title page: A page from Abraham Lincoln's Emancipation Proclamation, which declares that all slaves should be freed

Contents

1

Slavery (and Abolition) Begin

The first African people in the new English colonies in America were indentured servants, not slaves. Like white indentured servants, they worked for a number of years and then were freed. Once free, they could work, vote, buy and sell land, and appear in courts of law to defend their rights. By the late 1600s, black indentured servants in the North and South were becoming slaves.

★ **1619**
Twenty African settlers are brought to the British colony of Jamestown, Virginia.

★ **1640**
Three indentured servants run away from their Virginia master but are captured. The two white servants each have four years added to the term they must work. The black servant is sentenced to work the rest of his life.

★ **1641**
Massachusetts becomes the first colony to recognize slavery as legal.

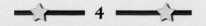

★ **1644**

Eleven blacks in New Netherlands (which later became the state of New York) petition the governor and are freed because they have completed the number of years of service agreed to.

★ **1662**

Virginia law says that children are born as slaves if their mothers are slaves.

★ **1682**

Virginia law says slaves cannot own weapons, leave their owner's plantation without permission, or defend themselves against a white person. Runaways can be killed if they resist capture. Slaves can be killed during punishment.

Above is a diagram of the slave ship *Brookes* showing the stowage, where the slaves were kept. The stowage was belowdecks and was very uncomfortable. There was space for 292 slaves on the lower deck. Another 130 slaves were crammed on shelves and around the edges of the deck. They had very little space.

Early Protests Against Slavery

Two groups were against slavery right away: members of the Society of Friends (also called Quakers) and the slaves themselves. Slaves fought for their freedom by escaping (and helping others escape), taking over the ships that brought them to the colonies, and rebelling against their

owners. Their rebellions caused slave owners to pass harsher laws controlling the slaves' behavior. Free blacks formed abolition societies—although a few bought slaves themselves. Quakers argued for an end to the slave trade and the gradual freeing of slaves.

This is an image of slaves on a slave ship who are revolting against their owners so they can be free. This kind of revolt is called a mutiny. The image is from the eighteenth century.

★ **1688**

The Quakers of Germantown, Pennsylvania, pass America's first antislavery resolution.

★ **1699**

Slaves mutiny at sea, taking over the slave ship that has captured them. This is the first of about fifty-five mutinies that will take place between 1699 and 1845.

Above, black slaves are being branded on the back. Some slaves were marked by their owners to indicate who they belonged to.

★ **1702**

Massachusetts judge Samuel Sewell publishes the first antislavery document in the colonies.

★ **1712**

Slaves in New York City revolt, killing nine people. Of the twenty-seven slaves captured, twenty-one are executed. Six kill themselves. Pennsylvania law forbids the importing of slaves. South Carolina law requires the branding of slaves who run away two times. For a third escape attempt, the slave would have his or her ear cut off.

★ **1713**

Quakers in Philadelphia make plans for freeing slaves, educating them, and returning them to Africa.

★ **1739**

Several groups of slaves revolt in South Carolina.

7

2
The American Revolution

The Declaration of Independence says, "We hold these truths to be self-evident [obvious], that all men are created equal and that they are endowed [given] by their Creator with certain inalienable [unquestionable] Rights, that among these are Life, Liberty and the pursuit of Happiness." Northern and southern colonies (they were not yet states) began a 100-year-long struggle to understand how a country founded on these "truths" could hold slaves.

★ **1772**
All slaves in England are freed, but England refuses to limit the sale of slaves in the colonies.

★ **1774**
Minister Richard Allen, a former slave, forms the antislavery African Methodist Episcopal Church in Philadelphia.

Minister Richard Allen

★ **1774**
Connecticut, Massachusetts, and Rhode Island ban the importing of slaves. Virginia passes a "resolution condemning slavery."

1775

The American Revolution begins.

1775

Anthony Benezet, a Quaker, forms the Society for the Relief of the Free Negroes Unlawfully Held in Bondage.

1776

Language condemning slavery is removed from the Declaration of Independence when some states object.

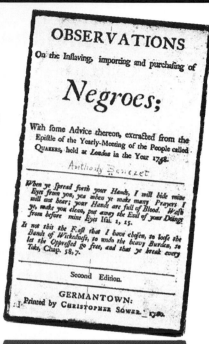

This is a title page from antislavery writings by Anthony Benezet.

1777

Vermont becomes the first state to outlaw slavery. By 1804, all states north of Delaware vote to end slavery, although some set a date in the future to end it.

1781

Elizabeth Freeman petitions the state of Massachusetts for her freedom. The Massachusetts Declaration of Rights says "all people are born free and equal." She is freed.

1783

The American Revolution ends. About 100,000 slaves are freed after the war or have escaped during it.

Slavery and the United States Constitution

In the United States Constitution, slaves and women did not have the rights promised by the Declaration of Independence. The new United States government could not agree to free the slaves. The states of Georgia, North Carolina, and South Carolina would not agree to a Constitution that banned slavery. The country's history would be shaped by the inability of the Founding Fathers to end slavery and by continued fears of slave revolts.

The United States Constitution (*left*) was written up in secret by delegates to the Constitutional Convention in the summer of 1787. They met in order to create the Constitution, which is a four-page document that discusses how the government of the United States should be run. It was signed on September 17, 1787.

★ 1784

Thomas Jefferson's proposal to ban slavery after 1800 is defeated by the Continental Congress.

★ 1787

The U.S. Constitution says that persons "held in service or labor escaping into another [state] ... shall be delivered up on the claim of that party to whom such service or labor may be due." That means that slaves must be returned to their owners. The Constitution also says that five slaves are equivalent to three free people when deciding how many congressional representatives each state would have. This gives slaveholders more power because their states will have extra congressmen in the House of Representatives. In the Northwest Ordinance, Congress says that slavery may not spread into the newly formed Northwest Territory.

Thomas Jefferson was born on April 13, 1743, at Shadwell Plantation in Virginia. This is a painting of him when he was secretary of state. Jefferson wrote the United States Constitution.

★ 1788–1792

Every state from Massachusetts to Virginia has at least one abolitionist society.

3

Slavery on the Rise

The Founding Fathers tried to limit slavery in the country, believing it would die out by itself as it was doing in the North. Virginia and Maryland had the most slaves who were needed for the cultivation of tobacco, but the land was becoming less fertile due to overplanting. South Carolina used slaves to grow rice, but the crop could only be grown near the coast. These are some of the reasons why, by the early 1790s, slavery was (temporarily) becoming less profitable.

In the South, slaves often had to pick cotton by hand. Then they would clean it. After Eli Whitney invented the cotton gin, slaves used the new machine. Even though it was a machine, the cotton gin had to be turned by hand, and it was tiring work.

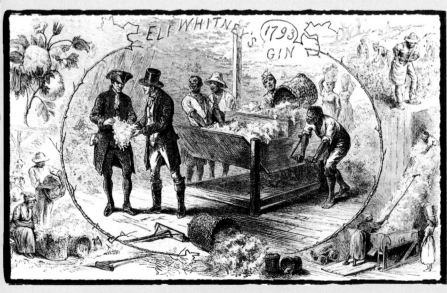

★ 1793

Eli Whitney patents the cotton gin, a machine that pulls the seeds from picked cotton. One person can now clean 50 pounds (22.7 kilograms) of cotton in one day. Before the gin, a person could clean only 1 pound (0.5 kg) a day. During this time, "king cotton" becomes the most important crop in the United States. As a result, slavery becomes more profitable than ever.

Eli Whitney

★ 1793

U.S. Congress passes the first federal Fugitive Slave Act. Slave owners can seize escaped slaves who have reached free states. Helping an escaping slave is made a crime. Free blacks are banned from Virginia.

★ 1794

Abolitionist societies of several northern and southern states hold a convention in Philadelphia.

★ 1800

Washington, D.C., replaces Philadelphia as the nation's capital. Slavery is legal in Washington.

★ 1803

President Thomas Jefferson buys the 885,000-square-mile (2,292,139-square-kilometer) Louisiana Territory from France.

The Colonization Movement

In the early 1800s, many white people wanted to send blacks back to Africa or to colonies in Haiti or elsewhere. They wanted to do this for many reasons. They hoped that this would stop the blacks from causing rebellions and that this opportunity would allow blacks a chance to have the freedom that they were not permitted in the United States. Another reason was that this would keep blacks from competing with white workers for jobs.

The Underground Railroad was a system set up to help slaves move to freedom in the North. This image shows escaped black slaves and the white people who helped them on Levi Coffin's farm in Indiana.

1808

The U.S. government bans the importing of slaves, but smuggling of slaves continues.

1816

The American Colonization Society is founded to send freed blacks to Africa.

1817

Blacks hold an anticolonization convention in Philadelphia. Participants argue that blacks born in the United States should have the rights promised by the Constitution.

1820

The United States Congress passes the Missouri Compromise. Missouri will join the United States as a slave state but Maine will be free. The compromise bans slavery in new territories north of Missouri's southern border. However, slavery now spreads to new states.

1822

Freeman Denmark Vesey begins a rebellion in Charleston intended to free all blacks in the region and kill all whites.

1827

Levi Coffin, a Quaker abolitionist, moves from North Carolina to Indiana to work on the Underground Railroad. By the 1820s and 1830s, "conductors" smuggle slaves along well-organized routes to free states and Canada.

4

From Antislavery to Abolition

The 1830s were the beginning of an explosive time. Many white people opposed to slavery had argued for a gradual end to it. White abolitionist William Lloyd Garrison wrote, "I do not wish to think, or speak, or write, with moderation … Tell a man whose house is on fire to give a moderate alarm … but urge me not to use moderation in a cause like the present … I will not retreat a single inch—AND I WILL BE HEARD."

★ **1829**
Freeman David Walker publishes *An Appeal to the Colored Citizens of the World* demanding immediate emancipation, no slave colonies, and full rights. He writes that violence may be necessary if slaves must "kill, or be killed."

　　Georgia passes a law outlawing literature, like Walker's *Appeal*, that might lead to a revolt.

★ **1831**
William Lloyd Garrison begins publishing the *Liberator*. He agrees with Walker's demands but is against the use of violence. Few whites agree with

LADIES' DEPARTMENT.

'Am I not a Woman and a Sister?'

White Lady, happy, proud and free,
Lend awhile thine ear to me ;
Let the Negro Mother's wail
Turn thy pale cheek still more pale.
Can the Negro Mother joy
Over this her captive boy,
Which in bondage and in tears,
For a life of wo she rears ?
Though she bears a Mother's name,
A Mother's rights she may not claim ;
For the white man's will can part,
Her darling from her bursting heart.

Below are two pages from an 1848 edition of David Walker's book, *An Appeal to the Colored Citizens of the World*. Walker was born in 1785 and died in 1830. At right is a photo of William Lloyd Garrison, taken between 1855 and 1865. Garrison joined the abolitionist movement when he was twenty-five. He became famous for the antislavery newspaper he wrote called the *Liberator*. The first issue was published in 1831 and the last issue was published in 1865. At left is a page from the *Liberator*.

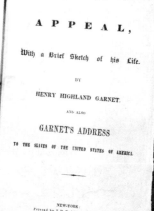

WALKER'S

A P P E A L,

With a Brief Sketch of his Life.

BY

HENRY HIGHLAND GARNET.

AND ALSO

GARNET'S ADDRESS

TO THE SLAVES OF THE UNITED STATES OF AMERICA

NEW-YORK
Printed by J. H. Tobitt, 9 Spruce-st.
1848.

him, but he angers pro-slavery people and encourages blacks, who are his earliest supporters. A slave preacher named Nat Turner leads a two-day revolt in which state troops kill many innocent blacks and local whites kill others.

Antislavery Societies and Their Enemies

Disagreements about slavery grew stronger through the 1830s and 1840s. Slavery continued to become more important economically and politically in the South, but northerners were not in agreement about abolition. Most white northerners still didn't want a large free black population, and northern states continued to limit the rights of free blacks.

This lithograph sought to expose the violence directed against those who supported the abolitionist movement in the South. A lithograph is a type of drawing that is made on stone and then printed.

1833
The American Anti-Slavery Society (AASS) holds its first meeting of sixty-three men, black and white, including William Lloyd Garrison. The AASS holds conventions, publishes books, and sends out lecturers. It urges boycotts of slave-produced products. Members pledge to petition Congress to end slavery in Washington, D.C.

1834
Antiabolition riots take place in New York City and Philadelphia.

★ **1835**

Southern states make it illegal for abolitionists to work or live in the South. President Andrew Jackson supports laws that ban the mailing of antislavery literature and encourages postmasters to search people's mail.

★ **1836**

Congress passes a gag rule: All antislavery petitions will be ignored by Congress. This is unconstitutional because the Constitution gives citizens the right to petition.

★ **1837**

A mob murders Elijah P. Lovejoy who has published antislavery editorials in his Illinois newspaper.

On the night of November 7, 1837, a mob, or angry crowd, attacked the warehouse of Elijah Lovejoy and Godfrey Gilman in Alton, Illinois. This image shows the mob setting fire to the warehouse.

★ **1838**

A mob burns Philadelphia Hall (where abolitionists are holding a meeting), a black orphanage, and a church.

5.

From Protest to Politics

Antislavery groups engaged in boycotts, protests, petitions, arguments, and violence. Beginning in the 1840s, group members ran for political offices. The need to attract large numbers of people to their cause caused disagreements among abolitionists. Some of these involved the place of women and blacks in abolitionist groups.

This illustration shows the slave uprising on the *Amistad*. The slaves had knives and fought against Captain Ferrer and his crew. Ferrer and the ship's cook were killed.

★ **1839**
Joseph Cinque leads fifty-three illegally captured blacks in the famous *Amistad* mutiny. They land the boat on Long Island, New York, and are arrested.

★ 1839

The Liberty Party, the first antislavery party, holds a convention in Warsaw, New York. Meanwhile, an abolitionist named Theodore Weld publishes *Slavery As It Is*. This includes speeches from southern congressmen and reports from southern news-papers. It becomes a best-seller.

★ 1840

William Lloyd Garrison adds women's rights to the causes that will be supported by the American Anti-Slavery Association. (At this time,

A painting of the convention of the American Anti-Slavery Society in 1840. The painting is by an artist named B. R. Haydon.

women, like slaves and many free blacks, cannot vote or own property.) He does not believe in voting or in elected officials and burns a copy of the United States Constitution because it legalized slavery. Abolitionist Lewis Tappan and about 300 others leave the AASS. Lucretia Mott and other women abolitionists take over leadership positions in the AASS.

★ 1841

The U.S. Supreme Court finds the *Amistad* mutineers innocent, and they are returned to their homes in Africa.

The Rise of Black Abolitionist Voices

The split between the North and the South continued to worsen. Southerners felt that their way of life was being attacked and feared slave uprisings. Northerners supported abolition for many reasons, including fear of economic competition from slaves. More northerners wanted to end slavery but at no time did the majority of northerners want blacks to have equal rights.

1841
Escaped slave Frederick Douglass addresses a convention of the Massachusetts Anti-Slavery Society.

1843
Sojourner Truth (born Isabelle Baumfree) becomes an abolitionist speaker. She had run away from her New York owner in 1827. She also supports women's rights and other social reforms.

Frederick Douglass

1844
The gag rule is voted down in Congress.

1845
Texas is admitted to the Union as a slave state. Frederick Douglass publishes *Narrative of the Life of Frederick Douglass*. He becomes a very powerful abolitionist.

★ **1846**

Slave hunters in Michigan are arrested for kidnapping, leading to the Fugitive Slave Act of 1850.

★ **1847**

Frederick Douglass begins publishing the *North Star*, an abolitionist newspaper, in Rochester, New York.

★ **1847–1848**

Virginia passes laws forbidding anyone to speak against slavery.

★ **1848**

Mexico loses the Mexican-American War and gives up a huge amount of land to the United States.

★ **1849**

Harriet Tubman escapes from slavery but returns to the South nineteen times as a conductor on the Underground Railroad. She helps free hundreds of people.

A photograph of Harriet Tubman in 1911 at her home in Auburn, New York. Tubman was born into slavery in 1819 or 1820, in Dorchester County, Maryland.

6

The Road to War

Many historians believe that the Compromise of 1850 made civil war unavoidable. The Fugitive Slave Act required that every northerner had to enforce slavery. The North and the South became more and more different economically. The North built factories and hired immigrants, and the South remained a farming region. However, only a quarter of southerners owned slaves.

A poster for the book *Uncle Tom's Cabin*. After it was published, the book became a best-seller. It has never been out of print. The author, Harriet Beecher Stowe, was born on June 14, 1811, in Litchfield, Connecticut. Stowe died on July 1, 1896, in Hartford, Connecticut.

★ 1850

The Compromise of 1850 states that California is a free state, but Utah and New Mexico (states created from land won in the Mexican-American War) will decide for themselves whether to be slave or free states. Slave trading (but not slavery) is ended in Washington, D.C. The Fugitive Slave Act causes many free blacks to be enslaved. About 20,000 northern blacks move to Canada.

★ 1852

Harriet Beecher Stowe publishes her best-selling novel, *Uncle Tom's Cabin,* about the horrors of slavery. This creates further outrage against the South.

Harriet Beecher Stowe

★ 1854

Congress passes the Kansas-Nebraska Act, allowing these new states to vote for or against slavery. The Missouri Compromise had made this region free. The Republican Party is founded in response to the Kansas-Nebraska Act. Its goal is to prevent the spread of slavery.

Escaped slave Anthony Burns is captured in Boston. For weeks, abolitionists and federal troops fight. A deputy is killed. Burns is the last person returned to slavery from Massachusetts.

The End of Slavery

When Abraham Lincoln was elected as the sixteenth president of the United States, he said, "I believe this government cannot [last] permanently half slave and half free." He believed slavery was wrong, but he did not promise to end it. Lincoln wanted to preserve the Union and avoid civil war, but the North and the South had run out of compromises. However, he eventually brought about the emancipation of slaves.

This is a nineteenth-century illustration of Abraham Lincoln (*seated, third from left*) reading the Emancipation Proclamation. The other men in the painting are his cabinet members.

1856

Abolitionist and pro-slavery forces fight in Kansas for four months, resulting in the deaths of about 200 people.

1857

The U.S. Supreme Court rules against slave Dred Scott. The Court says a slave does not become free when taken to a free state. The Court also says that Congress has no constitutional right to outlaw slavery in any state.

1859

White abolitionist John Brown raids the government arsenal at Harpers Ferry, Virginia. He and a group of men (black and white) are outnumbered by militia and U.S. troops before they can carry out his plan to lead a general uprising of black slaves.

1860

Abraham Lincoln is elected president. South Carolina secedes from the Union in December. More states follow in 1861.

1863

President Lincoln's Emancipation Proclamation frees all slaves in rebel territory.

1865

The Thirteenth Amendment to the U.S. Constitution out-laws slavery.

How Timelines Help You Learn

A timeline shows events and the dates when these events happened, beginning with the earliest and ending with the latest. It is a good way to get a quick idea about what happened during a certain period of time and how all the events fit together.

Timelines can also help us see how one event caused later ones. People who fought against slavery responded to laws made by England when America was an English colony and then to laws made by the United States government. The history of the United States includes many compromises between people who were against slavery and people who wanted it to continue.

Glossary

abolition (a-buh-LIH-shun) The official ending of slavery.

bondage (BAHN-dihj) Slavery; one person "owning" another person.

boycott (BOY-kaht) A refusal to deal with something, such as a company or product, as a protest against it.

compromise (KOM-pruh-myz) An agreement in which each side gets something it wants and gives up something it wants.

Continental Congress (kon-tin-EN-tul KON-gres) A political body that directed the American Revolution.

cultivate (KUHL-tih-vayt) To grow, as in, to cultivate tobacco.

Declaration of Independence (deh-kluh-RAY-shun UV in-duh-PEN-dints) An official announcement approved on July 4, 1776, in which American colonists stated they were free of British rule.

emancipate (ih-MAN-sih-payt) To free from slavery.

emancipation (ih-MAN-sih-pay-shun) The act of freeing slaves.

endowed (en-DOWD) To be granted with something.

gag rule (GAG RHULE) A rule stating that people cannot pass on important information.

indentured servant (in-DEN-churd SIR-vint) One who works for an agreed-upon period of time for payment in goods and/or lands.

A Timeline of the Abolitionist Movement

militia (muh-LIH-shuh) A group of people who are trained and
ready to fight in an emergency.

moderation (mah-duh-RAY-shun) Being within reasonable limits.

petition (puh-TIH-shun) A formal written request to an authority.
The right of the people to petition the government is guaranteed
by the U.S. Constitution.

resolution (reh-zuh-LOO-shun) An official statement of the ideas
of a group, voted on and put to use.

secede (sih-SEED) To withdraw from a group or a country. The
South seceded from the United States before the Civil War.

secession (sih-CEH-shun) The act of leaving a group.

uprising (up-RY-zing) A revolt or rebellion.

Web Sites

Due to the changing nature of Internet links, the Rosen Publishing
Group, Inc., has developed an online list of Web sites related to the
subject of this book. This site is updated regularly. Please use this
link to access the list.

http://www.rosenlinks.com/tah/abmo

Index

Credits

About the author: Judy Levin is a children's librarian and a freelance editor and writer living in New York City.

Photo credits: cover © North Wind Picture Archives; p. 1 © General Records of the United States Government/National Archives; p. 5 © Hulton Archive/Getty Images; pp. 6, 8, 12, 13, 14, 17 (left), 21, 26 © Bettmann/Corbis; pp. 7, 19 © Corbis; p. 9 © Library of Congress Rare Book and Special Collections Division; p. 10 © Records of the continental and Confederation Congresses and the Constitutional Convention, 1774-1789, Record Group 360/National Archives; pp. 11, 17 (middle and right), 18, 22, 23, 24, 25 © Library of Congress Prints and Photographs Division; p. 20 © Underwood & Underwood/Corbis.

Designer: Geri Fletcher; Editor: Annie Sommers